CHAPBOOKS

"circumgyrations"
In Case of Emergency Press, 2006

"More Fun With 'Pataphysics"
above/ground press, 2006

"Fun With 'Pataphysics"
bookthug, 2005

& online at *minimalist concrete*, 2006

ANTHOLOGIES

Young Poets' Anthology
Charlottesville: Outside Voices, forthcoming 2008
Editor: Jessica Smith

Shift & Switch: New Canadian Poetry
Toronto: The Mercury Press, 2005
Editors: a.rawlings, derek beaulieu, jason christie

AVATAR

For Ginevra!

I love you

SHARON HARRIS

THE MERCURY PRESS

2006

The publisher gratefully acknowledges the financial assistance of the Canada Council for the Arts, the Ontario Arts Council, the Ontario Media Development Corporation, and the Ontario Book Publishing Tax Credit Program. The publisher further acknowledges the financial support of the Government of Canada through the Department of Canadian Heritage's Book Publishing Industry Development Program (BPIDP) for our publishing activities.

Editor: Beverley Daurio
Cover art and design: Sharon Harris
Page design: Beverley Daurio and Sharon Harris

Printed and bound in Canada
Printed on acid-free paper

1 2 3 4 5   10 09 08 07 06

Library and Archives Canada Cataloguing in Publication

Harris, Sharon, 1972-
        Avatar / Sharon Harris.
Poems.
ISBN 1-55128-121-X
        I. Title.
PS8615.A7483A92 2006   C811'.6   C2006-904315-9

The Mercury Press
Box 672, Station P, Toronto, Ontario Canada M5S 2Y4
www.themercurypress.ca

Our poetry is written on computers.
Does that make Tao invalid?

— Deng Ming-Dao

ON WORLD W/ ARROW KEYS

INFORMATION TECHNOLOGY
IS NOT THE FUTURE

a place of takeoffs and landings
a private bedroom laboratory
sixteen pages of wildfire

the tale of tales, the making
of numbers

getting lost is part process/
part adam and eve quake models

collateral damage

   how to make love and destroy and get
         a proper burial   a new archival pag

           we navigate on world with arrow keys
               playing with your hand

00111001

Now

Silky Tendon Entity Playing Heaven Enough Now,
Junction On Side Ending Pain. Happy
Could Allow I Now.

Sexual Tantra Evolving Playful Hatha Enveloping Nothingness
Joining Ossa. Surrendering Evermore Pliancy Here —
Can Another Inch Nonresist?

Sequacious Talking Ending Places Hearing Emptiness Not
Jabber Only Spaces Expanding Pleasantly Holding
Cherished Adjectives Intending Now.

Sleep, Telling. Excogitations Possibly Heard Enter Night
Jumping Obtaining Speech Pandorically Heaving
Chest Afflinging Is Now.

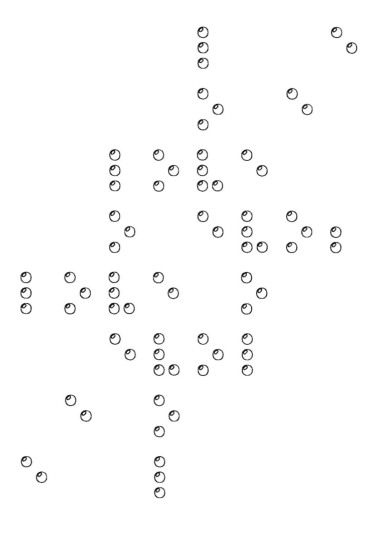

TRANSACTIONS OF AN INHABITANT

where you are
where i am
how we are both feeling

what is happening
what might happen
there is much to listen to

they ask questions
not like men
who know everything and don't read

you are driving home and
calling from the car
to say that   you are driving home

0011000100110010

FIGURE B

FIGURE C

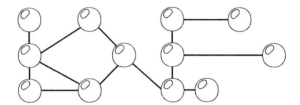

FIGURE D

FIGURE E

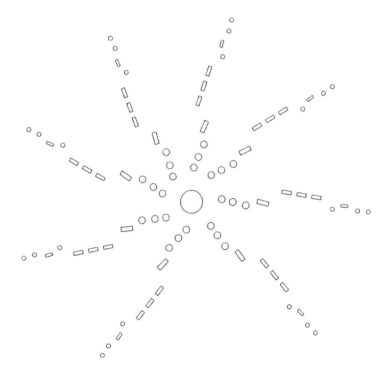

terrestrial planet finder

to search for family
portraits of stars,
their orbiting planets and determine
the mission:

from disks of dust
to homes for possible life/

wondering if they sleep

how to distinguish bodies
against the blinding glare
of their parents   warm up inside

collect starlight
and the dim light
reflected from planets

detect the faint spheres

0011000100110111

space policy

the angles of connections
shift   differ

skin turns
transparent

mapping
the coordinates
by which you act

nothing of colour
matters

it is the right
of every person

to stand and stare

across the barrens/
desolation of surfaces

   not the
   eyesore
   of crashes

scattered beyond
the landscapes

the noosphere drifts   blowing
us to worlds
like poems

on world w/ arrow keys

escape
backspace

insert home

tabulation delete
end

capitals
lock

enter
shift shift

control
alternate

space

alternate
control

0011000100111001

FIGURE F

FIGURE G

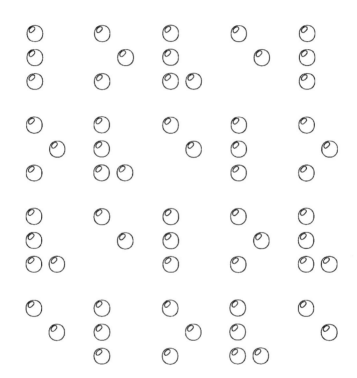

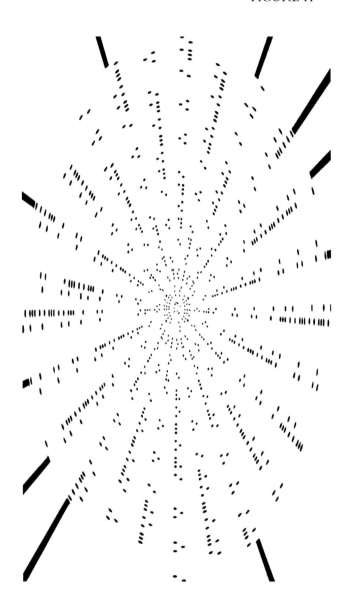

properties of the universe

two fingers separated by the body
        join with a single concept in the mind

imagination trajects reality
        every thought through every step

we get more out of it/
        than was originally put into it

love

is a poetry of superfluous words
        passion orbits the peripheries of symbols

we work hard to wrest something from nature
        delivering information like signposts

on the eighth day God made a blueprint of Her work
        a criterion for greatness

solve the problem that inspired your construction

it will fit on a t-shirt

0011001000110011

verse / version

7. finally, there is only soaring
1. you cannot go back one minute
1.1. or one day
2. the holiest words gradually lost their power
and constantly speak of returning
3.
4. everything you do is spontaneously correct
4.1. beginning
4.2. middle
4.3. end
4.4. start again
5. tell the secret of life ten times over and it is still
6. safe

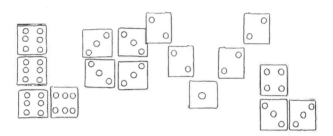

FIGURE I

a little peace here

a little peace there,

and pretty soon

all the little peaces fit together

to make one big peace

everywhere

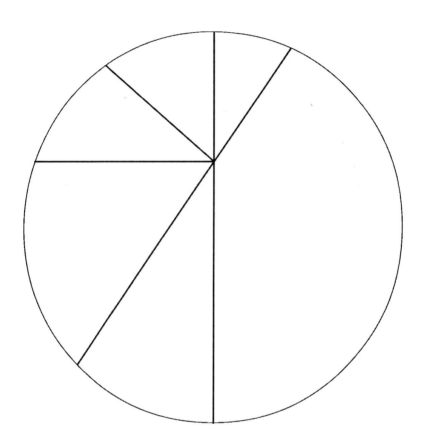

FUN W/ 'PATAPHYSICS

99a. WHERE DO POEMS COME FROM?

Moisten your finger and hold it straight up in the air. You will notice at once that one side of the finger is cold. This is the direction from which the poem is coming.

163. HOW DO I WRITE A HAPPY POEM?

Lay a piece of writing paper on a windowsill, and place a polished glass of water upon it. Tape a postcard with a pencil-width slit to its outside so that a ray of sunlight shines through, onto the water's surface. Bands of red, orange, yellow, green, blue, indigo and violet will form on the paper.

Pause to thank the sun, air and water. If you manage to keep your ego out of the rainbow you've created, then only happy words will assemble on the page. Congratulations! When you are finished, take a long draught of the water, and write an ecstatic chapbook.

163a. HAPPY POEMS

A happy poem is a natural phenomenon that causes a nearly continuous spectrum of light to appear in the sky. Its existence depends on the observer's location: that is, even on a sunny day, not everyone can see a happy poem.

Joy is part of poetry despite the poor ability of humans to distinguish it from lesser emotions. Sometimes we only manage a fleeting glimpse. Happiness in poems is often overlooked, and sadly mistaken for irony.

187. POET IN A BAG

Trap a poem in a smooth paper bag, seal it, and hold it horizontally above your ear. If you are in a quiet room you'll hear the patter of its metre quite clearly.

The paper behaves like the skin of a drum. Although only the tiny serifs of the letterforms beat upon it, it begins to vibrate and transmits quite a racket. You might imagine you've captured a poet in the bag.

227. CONFUSED WRITING

Would you bet that you cannot write a poem if you make circular movements with your leg at the same time? You will likely manage nothing more than an unreadable scribble.

Each action needs so much concentration that both cannot be carried out at the same time, but a minuscule percentage of poets thrives on futile exercises such as this. Be thankful you're not a concrete poet.

228. MISTAKE POEM

Rest a stiff leaf of paper on the front of your forehead, and try to write a poem upon it. You will be surprised at what appears. Since you have started writing at the left and finished at the right, your poem is backwards – readable only in the mirror.

'Pataphysics is the study of imaginary solutions, so you might want to transcribe each laterally reversed letter anyhow. When finished, translate into a language of your own invention.

332. FOR REVIEWERS

There is a very simple method for distinguishing a good poem from a bad one without hurting anyone's feelings. Rotate the poem in question on a plate, and the true masterpiece will spin in the mind for eons. If its form and content are uniformly distributed and mostly pure, then it will stay upright like a top.

The contradictions within a lesser work prevent this. Since the form and content are likely warring, these opposing forces create a sense of inertia. Thus, the poem falls flat, and doesn't stand up to the force of reviewing.

254. MUSE IN A BOTTLE

Fill a small goblet to overflowing with dried words, pour in Canadian Whiskey to the brim, and place the glass on a metal lid. As the words fill and expand, their internal pressure increases until a force similar to that of a jackhammer is created.

The heap of words becomes slowly higher and then a clatter of falling poems begins, which goes on for hours.

162. AN UNCUTTABLE POEM

Place a folded poem around a knife blade. You can cut a reader with it without damaging the poem.

The poem is forced into the reader with the knife. It is not cut itself because the pressure of the blade on the poem is countered by the resistance from the reader. Since the reader's flesh is softer than the poem fibre, it yields. If, however, you hold the poem too firmly, the pressure balance is lost, and the poem is broken.

123. WATER POEM

Cut out a poem shape from smooth writing paper, colour it with crayons, and fold the petals firmly inward. If you place the poem on water you will see the petals open in slow motion.

Poems consist mainly of word fibres, which are composed of extremely fine tubes. The water fills these so called capillary tubes, causing the poem to swell and the letters of the poem to open up, like the leaves of a wilting plant when it is placed in water.

41. IF I PLACE A POEM AND ITS TRANSLATION ACROSS
FROM EACH OTHER, AND I STAND BETWEEN THEM,
CAN I SEE MY REFLECTION STRETCHING AWAY
INTO INFINITY?

In theory, you could get an infinite number of reflections in the
poems, but only if the poem was perfectly translated and you
stood there forever.

70. WHY DO POEMS MAKE ME CRY?

Reading a poem releases noxious gases into your environment. The brain reacts by telling your tear ducts to produce water, to dilute the irritating acid so the eyes are protected. Your other reaction is probably to rub your eyes, but this will make the aggravation a lot worse if you have poem essence all over your hands.

There are various kinds of remedies for dealing with this annoying phenomenon — some more effective than others. As a general rule, move your head as far away from the poem as you can, so the gas will mostly disperse before it reaches your eyes. The simplest solution might be not to date poets.

124. EDITING POEMS

Fill a tall jar with water and place your latest poem in it. Try to drop words into the text. It is very surprising that however carefully you aim, the words nearly always slip to the side.

It is seldom possible to get a word to fall straight. The very slightest nuance with even the smallest tilt is enough to cause a greater resistance of the water on the slanting underside of the word. Because words are full of holes, they turn easily and drift out of context.

92. I'VE WRITTEN A POEM. HOW DO I GET IT PUBLISHED?

Write the poem and your name on a tulip bulb. Plant the bulb in the earth and when the tulip blooms, so shall your poem.

48. WHY DO POEMS SPARKLE?

Even if a poem looks rough, some of its very small parts can be smooth as a mirror. When light hits something smooth, it bounces. The more smooth parts the light has to bounce off, the more it sparkles. So poems with lots of little smooth bits really sparkle and shine.

7. LOST POETS

Why do poets fly to the warm lights of pubs and bars? They are not naturally attracted to these places, but misled. Flying at night, poets steer by the moon. They know they are flying in a straight line as long as the moon shines into their eyes from the same side. But when they pass the lights of a public house (on the other side), they get confused. They leave their straight flight path and approach in spirals.

34. THE GREAT CANADIAN SOUND POEM

If you have dry, frizzy hair, wear glasses and have a pine tree you can lean against the next time the Northern Lights are in the sky, you might hear some Canadian sound poetry.

How? Your hair and the needles of the pine tree vibrate to the very low frequency sounds given off by the lights. With luck, your ears will turn these vibrations into sound poems. Your glasses help boost the sound as they transfer the vibrations directly to the bones in your head.

0011010000110110

292. HOW TO SCARE POETS

A poet's eye is attracted instinctively by shining objects. A poet looks for any round, light-coloured things, such as the eggs of a songbird, which it steals out of the nest.

Take one of the bright balls used for Christmas decorations, close it at the top with a waterproof adhesive, and fasten it to a post or a tree in the garden where it may be seen from all sides. The reflection of the sun on the ball will follow the suspicious poet into every corner of the garden and irritate it so much that it will fly away.

EXPERIMENTS IN PROGRESS

Can I get warts from touching a poet? Do poets dream?

If I swallow my words, will they stay in my stomach for ten years?

Is life its own metaphor?

If a sound poet makes a funny face, will it be stuck forever?

How many poems would I have to write for the total to add up to $16?

0011010000111000

111. WHY SHOULD I NOT FREEZE A POEM?

There is no reason that you should not freeze a poem that I am aware of.

VIRUS

FIGURE K

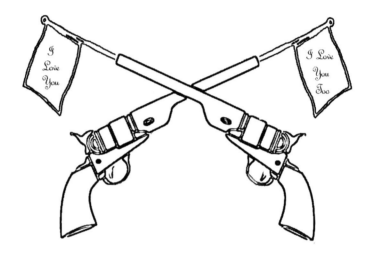

FIGURE L

I[1] Love[2] You[3]

0011010100110101

```php
<?php
echo "i love you";
?>
```

FIGURE M

I LOVE YOU WANTS TO BE FREE

It is suspected that a 23 year old man living in Manilla created I Love You.

Over a five hour period, during May 4 2000, I Love You spread across North America, Europe and Asia.

One DJ in Texas received I Love You 1500 times, but I Love You will most likely come from someone you know.

I Love You was blamed for shutting down the website of Florida's state lottery.

An alias of I Love You is Very Funny.

The State Department, the CIA, and the Defense Department said they had been hit by I Love You, but top security had not been breached.

I Love You affects your machine.

"People think of I Love You as an invasion from Mars," one researcher said, "my aim is to change people's attitudes, to cut down some of the fear."

Don't execute I Love You. You will be fine.

BIZARRE LOVE TRIOLET

1.

i love you
she said i love you
you really do love you

he loves you

really they love you
i so love you
really love you

we said we love you

0011010100111000

2.

i'm sorry
she said i'm sorry
you really are sorry

   he's sorry

really they're sorry
i'm so sorry
really sorry

   we said we're sorry

0011010100111001

LOVE-LETTER-FOR-YOU.TXT.VBS

★ Here's a poem for you
★ I've written a poem for you
   ★ Love poems for you :)
★ Look what I wrote for you
   ★ Poems for you

★ LovePoem
★ Poem_collection
★ Zipped_poems
★ My Poems

★ Sad Stories and
★ My Story
★ Only poems
   ★ Poems for you

0011011000110000

FIGURE N

FIGURE O

FIGURE P

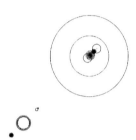

LINE IN | LINE OUT —

A-Line

"There are no such things as lines."

— *Buckminster Fuller*

startinglineinclinebeelineairlinelifelineonlineoutlinephonelinetime

0011011000110111

netalklinepencillinedottedlinethephiladephiatrentonlineassemblylinesightlinepartylinelinebyline

0011011000111000

badlineborderlinebanklinebankingmachinelinegoodlinebloodlineforgottenlineenlinehotlineba

0011011000111001

ontlinefoullinebluelineredlinegoallinethethinredlinebotomlineout of linecheckoutlinetowline

0011011100110000

icallinespringlinesummerlinefalllinewinterlinedeclinefinishline

0011011100110001

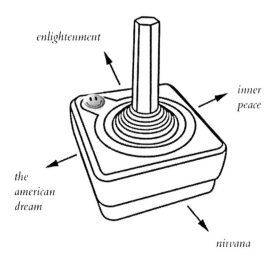

enlightenment

inner peace

the american dream

nirvana

FIGURE Q

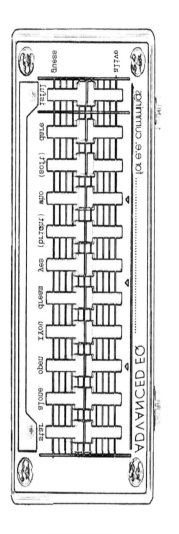

FIGURE R

white_lines

for Agnes Martin

"Let every line be its own revelation."
　— Edward Hirsch

the v's of pond behind a swimming duck
a cross section of a page
flight patterns of faeries flickering
the white stripe that lives when you're gone

a trail of puff after a plane
the spark of a panic attack
swishes and swooshes and starting flags
a printer streaking blank in text

a line of light beneath the bedroom door
a lie from conception to spoken
a ghost of cocaine　　shorter and shorter
guitar strings from the heavens

the heartline on the hand of a fetus
a missing ring　　fading to tan
the flash of an old god's fury
the white bone

toothy smiles from the blur of a toddler
spokes in the dharma wheel
the entire spectrum in the arc of an eyelash
the death of another ego

0011011100110100

FIGURE S

 us

them

SALUTOGENESIS

e

a

i

o

u

FIGURE T

u

UH
base
red
testes/ovaries
Aries
coccygeal
smell
structure
Padmasana
780 – 630 nanometers
tribe
primordiality
invigoration
action
national anthems
earth
material world
sexuality
Shekhinah
family
lust
justice
obsession
tribe
depression
garnet
patchouli
mars
iron
snake
stability
4
petals
deep C
All is one.

0011100000110000

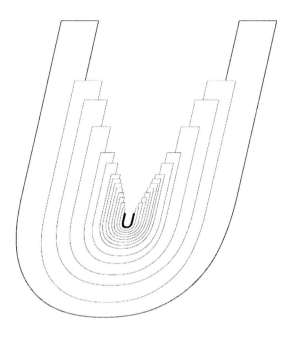

FIGURE U

0

OH
solar plexus
yellow
pancreas
Leo
ego
lumbar
sight
Bhujangasana
600 – 570 nanometers
expansion
creativity
personality
feelings
appearance
ethics
secrets
esteem
wisdom
rejection
risk
movement
digestion
discipline
ambition
character
criticism
topaz
Nezah Hod
sage
sun
bird
10 petals
E
Honour oneself.

0011100000110010

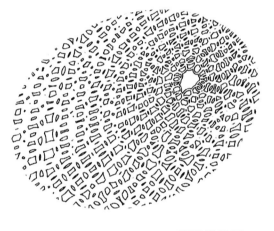

FIGURE V

i

EYE
heart
cyan
thymus
Scorpio
thoracic
touch
Virabhadrasana
550 – 520 nanometers
love
bitterness
compassion
hate
inspiration
loneliness
selflessness
healing
abandonment
fear
forgiveness
circulation
passion
hope
trust
despair
dedication
devotion
emerald
commitment
rose
venus
Tif'eret
copper
mammals
12 petals
G
Love is divine power.

FIGURE W

a

AY
brow
indigo
pituitary
Aquarius
brain stem
ESP
Nataraja Asana
500 – 450 nanometers
deepening clairvoyance
ordination
shadow
intelligence
intuituion
detachment
Binah Hokhmah
meditation
mind
memories
purification
diamond
frankincense
uranus
spirit guides
sinus infections
inner eye
duality
clairvoyance
mediums
lapis lazuli
visualization
clarity
silver
2 or 96 petals
A
Seek only the truth.

0011100000110110

FIGURE X

e

EEE
crown
white gold purple
pineal
Pisces
grace
fore
brain
all senses
Bakasana and Sirasana
450 - 380 nanometers
faith
transition
contemplation
unity
enlightenment
release
beingness
Keter
Extreme Unction
prophecy
mysticism
transcendence
divine
double helix
vortex
purity
gateway
ylang-ylang
neptune
prayer
platinum
1000 petals
B
Live in the present moment.

0011100000111000

FIGURE Y

I Feel So Good

today   trans beautiful strong
high fresh confident excellent
jump skip together when in
and the this gift by no with
a lift sun if or to too my !?

bike feel find give tree eat go
can climb energy ing ish est
laugh look love make walk
health share taste touch trust
we us she you run see play is

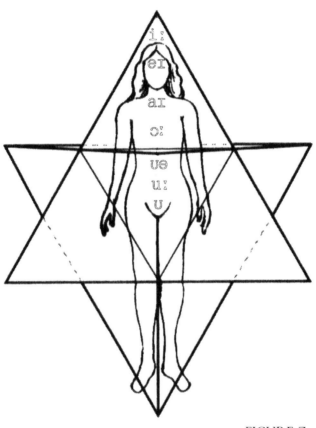

FIGURE Z

POETIC METHOD

Student Name Haceis   Date 14/12/2004

POETIC METHOD FORM

Question:

what is the radius of Goddess?

Hypothesis:

life is love is art is science is everything   there are less
than six degrees of separation

Method:

i) sampling ii) fine black markers iii) translations
within a language eg. love⟨⟩ : : : . ` language
echoing shadowing illuminating language
iv) breastfeeding

Results:

i take metaphor literally and can't tell if you're
teasing

Conclusion:

inconclusive

Manifest O

"If the first casualty of war is truth, the weapon of choice for its destruction is language." — Barrett Watten

Truth always gets destroyed by language — not just in war. Studies show that body talk is more dependable than words.

The body knows.

Language is a device of the left brain which tries to explain what the right brain already understands. Knowing sometimes gets lost when translated into words. The left brain doesn't always get it *right*.

Even my beloved I Love You — which I think is the most useful sentence in our language and closest to truth — is a lie. I don't believe that You and I are separate. We're Love. Sartre said,

"The other is hell."

When you love someone, you know how he feels. Love opens you to new ways of communicating that require less words. The writer's struggle to find the right word is famous, but there are no right words.

Consider the way you communicate with a lover. Or the way a mother communicates with her unborn child. Or the experiments that show how twins communicate with each other. Fewer words. No words (a lover can lie with words, but the loved one will either recognize the lie or spend a lot of energy in denial. Our children instantly know when we lie to them). We don't feel separate from each other in these relationships because the connections are palpable: lovers physically join together as one, the fetus and mom inhabit one body, and twins spend nine months together in close quarters. We feel part of the one.

There is a word for this way of communicating: telepathy. But it's more like empathy. We all know this space; we get to it by loving. It's not a failure to find words. It's the entrance to a new consciousness.

If you love everyone, you will know how everyone feels. If everyone loves you, everyone will know how you feel. It is where we're heading. A lot of cultures we called "primitive" or "pre-literate" are already there.

I'm not saying that the word is dead or that words aren't beautiful (there's a little bit of truth in everything). I think we'll need more words until we feel safe enough to go into the silence together. If we each practise loving everyone, we'll get there.

Until then,

I Love You.

LIST OF FIGURES (A - Z)

AVATARA

The Avatara, or incarnation of Godhead, descends from the kingdom of God. When They descend to the material creation, They assume the name Avatara.

— *The Vedas (Chaitanya-caritamrita 2.20.263 - 264)*

AVATAR

1. Among people working on virtual reality and cyberspace interfaces, an "avatar" is an icon or representation of a user in a shared virtual reality.

— *The On-line Hacker Jargon File 4.2.0*

NOTES ON THE TEXT

COVER AND SECTION PAGES

As the story goes, God said "Let there be light." From light came worlds. The planet drawings were digitally created from the colourful circles of light that splash across photos in certain lighting conditions.

Some people believe the lens flares accurately depict beings from a higher realm: therefore, the orbs of light are nicknamed "angels."

ON WORLD W/ ARROW KEYS

"Blues" is a Braille-inspired translation of bpNichol's "love" lattice of the same title and was Brailled by the Canadian National Institute for the Blind. "Spirally Agitated" is a translation of three works by bpNichol, Darren Wershler-Henry, and Steve Venright. "Circumgyrations" is a possible detail diagram of Braille characters. Two Morse Code poems: "A Little Peace Here" is PEACE (and a quote by Swami Beyondananda),. "Irreducibility" is Morse code for LOVE. "Peace *2.0*" spells P E A C E, not N D. The section includes an acrostic, a song, a prayer of keyboard commands and text copied/pasted from the Internet; it is heavily influenced by two years of MIT's *Technology Review.*

FUN W/ 'PATAPHYSICS

$$\text{``}\infty - \alpha + \alpha + 0 = \infty\text{''}$$
— Alfred Jarry

Fun W/ 'Pataphysics gives definitive answers to your unanswerable poetic questions and offers all the unsolicited writing advice you will never follow. For ages zero to aethernity.

VIRUS

"When someone says, 'I love you' and means it, it opens up
his throat — it literally does. And when the throat opens up,
so does the cervix. I've been checking a lady's dilation at the
same time she would say that, and I could feel a distinct
difference in her tissue, in how stretchy it was, that was exactly
synchronous with her saying, 'I love you.'" — Ina May Gaskin,
Spiritual Midwifery

"6 x 9" is a translation of Stephen Cain's "5 x 4 / 4 x 5"
sequence of poems. The foot-noted I Love You is a translation
of Natalee Caple's "In the Tunnels". "Love-Letter-For-
You.txt.vbs" was written using reported aliases of the I Love
You virus. Another alias for "I Love You" was "Very Funny."

SALUTOGENESIS

"Vowels are an expression of the divine (so sacred that
they were once only spoken by priests). Consonants are
an expression of humanity." — Patricia Mercer, *Chakras*

It is said that all knowledge and human experience is recorded
in the Akashic Records. The records resemble a library and
have also been compared to a universal computer (the "Mind
of God"). Some say we can access this collective mind through
our chakras. Each chakra is associated with a vowel sound:
each vowel is a potential portal.

A is for Christian, E is an intuitive map of the internet (a
flower of life), I is a collaboration with Garnett, O is my
favourite letter of the alphabet, and U is for you.

ACKNOWLEDGEMENTS

The author gratefully acknowledges the assistance of the Toronto Arts Council for financial support towards the completion of this project.

For your courage, grace and expertise: wholehearted gratitude to Beverley Daurio and a.rawlings at The Mercury Press.

For endless love: thank you, saint even.

AVATAR would not have been possible without: the Harris, Kerby, Hooper, and Martin families, Stewart Whitehead, Jay and Hazel MillAr, Nancy O'Connor, Bill Kennedy, Lee Pittaway, Stuart Ross, Christine Hooper, Betty and Ross Kerby, Adam Vaughan, Maggie Helwig, Michael Tweed, Ginevra Saylor, derek beaulieu, Christian Bök, John Barlow, Jon Paul Fiorentino, Max Fawcett, Mike, Joan and Anne Cain, Edward Keenan, Mark Truscott, Gregory Betts, Hugh Thomas, rob mclennan, Margaret Christakos, Dino Malito, Maria Erskine, Nathan Reimer, Steve Venright, Nadia Halim, Ron Nurwisah, Lisa Robertson, John Schmidt and the Schmidt family, Dan Waber, Lorrayne Anthony, Michael Ondaatje, Tess Malone, Suzanne Zelazo, Min Roman, Jackie Shawn, Charlie Huisken, Dooney's Café, the Mountview Community, the spirits of Agnes Martin, Alfred Jarry, and bpNichol, and the trees in High Park.

In the process of preparing this manuscript, the author's work appeared in *Word: Canada's Magazine for Readers + Writers, Geist, dANDelion, RAMPIKE, filling Station, Jacket Magazine, Quill & Quire, The National Post, The Capilano Review, Broken Pencil, hat, sudden magazine, Vallum,* housepress's *openpalmseries, Psychic Rotunda, Queen Street Quarterly,* and *eye weekly.* Visual pieces were shown at The Scream Literary Festival's Eyescream (Exhibitions I, III, and IV), the Toronto Free Gallery and on CityTV. Chapbooks were produced by bookthug, In Case of Emergency Press, above/ground press, and online at *minimalist concrete.* Seven poems were anthologized in *Shift & Switch: New Canadian Poetry.* Thanks to the curators, editors and publishers.

Special thanks to Emma, Cooper, Jasmine, Thomas, Reid, and Cole. Play is poetry.

This book is for Stephen, Cyan, and Garnett.

ABOUT THE AUTHOR

Sharon Harris is a writer and artist living in Toronto. Her work has appeared in magazines, literary journals, and newspapers, and on radio and television across Canada.

She is currently working on an illustrated book that is an unscientific study of the words "I Love You." Her online home is http://iloveyougalleries.com.